MW00737390

MEASURES

Nadya Aisenberg

salmonpoetry

Also by Nadya Aisenberg

Invincible Summer, Poems. Timberline Press, 1979. Fulton, Missouri.

A Common Spring: Crime Novel and Classic. Bowling Green
  Popular Press, 1979. Bowling Green, Ohio.

The Justice-Worm, Poems. Rowan Tree Press, 1981.
  Boston, Massachusetts.

London Crimes: Short Stories by Charles Dickens, edited and with
  a preface by Nadya Aisenberg. Rowan Tree Press, 1982.
  Boston, Massachusetts.

Women of Academe: Outsiders in the Sacred Grove.
  University of Massachusetts Press, 1988. Amherst, Massachusetts.
  (Co-authored with Mona Harrington).

We Animals: Poems of our World. Edited and with essays by Nadya Aisenberg.
  Sierra Club Books, 1989. San Francisco, California.

Before We Were Strangers, Poems. Forest Books, 1989. London.

Ordinary Heroines: Transforming the Male Myth. Continuum Press,
  1994. New York.

Leaving Eden, Poems. Forest Books, 1995. London.

Published in 2001 by
Salmon Publishing Ltd,
Cliffs of Moher, Co. Clare, Ireland
http://www.salmonpoetry.com
email: info@salmonpoetry.com

ISBN 1 903392 07 1   Paperback

Cover photography by Ilsa Thielan
Cover design and typesetting by Siobhán Hutson
Printed by Offset Paperback Mfrs., PA

Unfortunately, because this manuscript is being published posthumously, no personal acknowledgement or dedication exists.

Katy Aisenberg, Alan Aisenberg

Acknowledgements

The following poems were published individually, under titles, sometimes in a slightly different version:

1. The poem beginning: 'Here are the deliberations of the heart', *The Southern Poetry Review*, Winter 1997

2. The poem beginning: 'The formless needs to be concealed', *Poetry Magazine*, Summer 1996

3. The poem beginning: 'Of what is matter made', *Milkweed Anthology of Poetry on Math and Science*, 1997

4. The poem beginning: 'Sometimes I think everything that has happened', *Poetry London Newsletter*, Spring 1997

5. The poem beginning: 'It's not just energy, action, or even...', *The Ledge*, Spring 1997

6. The poem beginning: 'The snowflake falls heedlessly toward dissolution', *The Ledge*, Spring 1997

7. The poem beginning: 'Let us forsake footnotes', Honorable Mention, T. Nelson Gilbert Poetry Prize, 1997, *Woman in the Moon*

8. The poem beginning: 'As in the darkness there are unborn stars', *Poetry Review*, London, April 1997

9. The poem beginning: 'Agnes Martin paints the innocence', *Ekphrasis*, Summer 1998

10. The poem beginning: 'The woman knows she is not a metaphor', *Montserrat Review*, Fall 1998

11. The poem beginning: 'We scan the sky', *Quantom Tao*, Blue Heron Press 1998/ Winner Firman Houghton Prize, New England Poetry Society, 1998

12. The poem beginning: 'Was this what Michelangelo meant', *Birmingham Review*, December 1998

Contents

CALIBRATIONS

Constantly Describing Itself   3
Enlightenment   4
At The Other Chapel   5
Today   6
July, Maine   7
Lauds   8
The Singer   9
Almost Silence   10
Treviso   11
Advice   12
Feelings As Objects, Objects as Feelings   13
The Day The Horizon Disappeared   14
The Task   15
Hands   16

MEASURES

'Let us forsake footnotes...'   21
'The wilderness within...'   23
'*The universe, of which nature is the body,*
        God the soul...'   24
'But what of the planets' imperfect ellipses...'   25
'We rest our souls in Plato's Meadow,...'   26
'Of what is matter made...'   27
'The snowflake falls heedlessly toward dissolution...' 28
'Agnes Martin paints the innocence...'   29
'The formless needs to be concealed....'   30
'Like the excited atoms of the candle flame...'   31

'As in the darkness there are unborn stars,...'   32
'Sometimes I think everything that has happened...'   33
'The night gathers and advances...'   34
'Here are the deliberations of the heart:...'   35
'Zen leaves the circle,...'   36
'Seeking order on earth, we scan the sky,...'   37
'Sometimes you shrink from touch...'   38
'As brain-waves smooth out during sleep,...'   39
'There seems an interval between notes...'   40
'It's not just energy, action, or even de-centering...'   41
'Between the particle and the wave...'   42
'What is negotiable in this world?...'   43
'Perhaps we're standing on sacred dust,...'   44

Calibrations

Constantly Describing Itself

The red Virginia soil colors the rain
puddles red so they can't reflect the sky.
Everything that lives strives for color,
Goethe said. Not true. I strive for no-color,
no-sound, whatever can take me unto itself
in the singular steps of withdrawal,
erasure a kind of absolution
from the mind's thin repetitions.

There is too much blankness in the world
to be charged to inscribe, yet no one
waits for words, not the upturned faces
with open mouths, words are not their manna.
They wait to be claimed by some spirit
of devotion, to be rid of the self,
as waves and clouds appear
and disappear, never the same one twice.

Enlightenment

Who can believe in labels, periods,
Classical, Romantic, Modern,
since there's always the pre- and the post-
not to mention the influence of-

and the blustery wind of the past
knocks down the present while the future
is tapping her foot. So the good new days

resemble the good old days, and what
you count is war. O brave Enlightenment,
most certain of yourself, as if, turning

the charred pages of the text of history,
you could come upon one white page, undefaced,
on which to blaze your *Ode To Joy.*

Alles Menschen Werden Brüder.
As if that verb, imperative, would unfurl
itself through time, among the children foraging in ruins.

We suffer one another. Witness the vanishing
arcs of swallows as they swoop before dark,
the pine branch laden with snow, its beautiful burden,
a hand holding one white worshipful flower
between forefinger and thumb.

At The Other Chapel

Was this what Michelangelo meant, why he left
the few blue empty inches
between God's outstretched arm and Adam's hand?
Not the raised arm taking leave
of its creation, but the arm's refusal
to reach, to touch, the endless withholding?
Did the painter see his rosy, firm-fleshed
innocent doomed to awaken from his dream,
find time invented, the animals
quite happy without their names?
                              Sometimes the idea
is the measure of all things. We say
Light, say Love, call God the name
unnamable. Wanting even a spider's
web across that unspanned blue.
Sometimes the absence of God is God enough.

Today

Sailing home from the Barred Islands today
we saw two dolphins in tandem flash
That was enough for today
and tomorrow

July, Maine

As Shirtail Point this morning
29 geese and I swam alone
in cool translucent water
it was like a christening
a quiet joy
rippling to the opposite shore
where I stepped out into my real name
into the living present
which the geese and the solitude
made into a kind of grace
though they did not seem
like messengers
and the sky blue blue blue all the way home
the geese winging into it
messenger-wings on my feet

Thick summer afternoons, opening
into each other like the cells
of a honeycomb, hidden
under golden gaze, a faint hum
working the margins
days demanding nothing, like the homely
flowers ringing them, oxtail daisies,
Queen Anne's lace, yarrow,
names sweet on the tongue
the gifts we are given
make us cherish ourselves

Lauds

I was happy today, without knowing why,
the snow falling, still falling, going about
its layering, the dun fields a miraculous white.
My legs crampless, able to walk, words coming
with the rush of disembodied wind.
I scattered seeds for the birds who struggle
in the beauty that attaches me to this world.
The words and the snow coming together
as a perishable gift,
both changing the shape of the real,
filling it in,
as the sixty-eight churches of Moscow
before they burned
filled in the air with their peals
falling like words in the snow.

The Singer

The woman knows she is not a metaphor.
Not a willow, pliant, sad, leaning
toward water and her own reflection.
Nor is she the moon, cold distant
object of interperate desire. The self
may not know its own shape, whether
the sum of all the pointillist dots,
or the barely perceptible spaces between them.

She believes in the power of spirits,
magic, as in abduction, seduction,
the need to imagine the ugly as part
of the beautiful, for her hands to caress
the skin of all things. She remembers
how she kissed a Frog into a Prince,
handsome in green doublet and hose.

Can a self be chosen, inscribed,
the way a photographer fixes a subject
so there's no need to ask: Who am I today?

The woman remembers a moment,
a child tossing rhymes in the air,
learning, before she can write,
the incantation of words,
how they came from inside the body
to settle around her like birds,
some on her shoulders, some
pecking sounds from her hand,
how they'd return to sing
the longing she felt
as she sat on the steps
of the west-facing house
watching the sun sink the day.

Almost Silence

At night the dreams that are stored in the earth
rise up like groundmist, seeking their sleepers,
each to each, and enter silently, as they will depart.

And the sleepers who talk in their dreams utter
no sound, though something new is made, mist
condensing to image, a resolution we lose when we wake.

All speech tends towards silence, Goethe said, and so
the dream, strewing its path with misted grass, returns
through the humus of memory down

to the storehouse of dreams. Mist burns off in sun.
In the morning lips that were silent and wise
speak only to those who walk above ground.

Treviso

We are caught between stasis and motion,
the desire to hold, to belong, to be moored,
the dream of a harbor – and the dream of escape,
to be there, elsewhere, where we are out of ourselves.
And this is the sum of our lives, and our fretting.
Between silence and speech, pulling back, leaning out.
Like a small happiness afraid to be born,
not trusting the fastness of its roots in the earth
or if it will reach the blossoming air.

That afternoon in Treviso, caught in the rain,
just like Hollywood stars we chance into a bistro
with grilled prawns for lunch and know we are happy,
suspended in time between *goodbye* and *hello*.

The rain pings on the window, I could be that woman
hurrying home to make escarole soup. You'd be
my lover, ringing the doorbell with freesias and wine.
My pulse beats with the rhythm of music, of stars.

Advice

Friends, leave off the argy-bargy.
I don't believe terseness is all
but: There's bad and there's worse,
and either way, there's no time
for the mingy, doing the dirty,
lame-hearted grievance.
There's cold and there's freezing.
Now wrap your tongue
around something to love.

Feelings As Objects, Objects as Feelings

I see the black boulder hanging in the sky,
the lion dozing on the wardrobe.
You didn't have to go to such lengths,
a slight nudge would knock me off my perch.
I've already colonized terror, my eye alert
to any shift in angle, displacement,
twitch of a tail. Peripheral vision
tells me there's no safe place. These huge
projections of anxiety are overkill:
I habitually walk on tiptoe, whisper.

And when the lion doesn't pounce,
the boulder doesn't fall
you've used up your days
in the anteroom of hell.

The Day The Horizon Disappeared

Cast out, flung to the furthest rim of neediness,
then caught there in the branches of the danger tree,
where meaning dwells, out of reach, attached
on its green stem at the very edge of dreaming,
a sign repeating itself through branches
surging in air. Wind surrounds and blows through us.
And whose hand is tearing strips from the sky,
And whose hand will seed wild grasses
on the worn nap of the threadbare world?

The Task

The body shuts its pleasures down
like a shopkeeper in an occupied land
whose empty shelves attest:
There's nothing left to buy.

Death scoops up our friends,
a cow-catcher clearing the rails
for those riding behind.
Fewer to love, be loved by.

I tremble to see
your mouth slacken
while you sleep.

The task of paring, paring,
as if the past owned everything
but memory: our captive,
still-fleet selves, green shoots
through winter bark.

The time is now. The skittering mind
skims wave-fields,
Take hold, take hold.
A sparrow's dart and peck, bough quivering,
alight, flight.
And the cumbrous body below,
comforter-shroud wrapped like a presentiment
of that eternal heaviness we migrate to.

Who's living my beautiful life,
eating the sun, drinking the lashings of rain?

Hands

The artist has a hand inside the mind.
The hands outside collect the stones, paste
the feather, smooth the linen,
cut the copper, squeeze the paint,
hold the charcoal. The hands outside
are flesh, but the hand inside is will,
wanting to make it whole. Make what whole?
Itself, you, me, a grandiose proposition,
but nevertheless, if pressed, it will admit
to this. Insight of inside. The hand paints
itself inside the mind like a cave drawing,
powerful, primitive, red, an icon bringing
beasts to it for food, dispelling dangers.
The hand inside breaks up the light
in its fist, tesserae gleaming in darkest December
like the stained glass windows of cathedrals.
The story gradually emerges, the hands outside
working, moving, the hand inside staying quite still,
knowing the end of the story, then lifting the cup of wine,
making the sign of blessing, calming the anxious outside pair.

Measures

Measures

i.

Let us forsake footnotes
and the compilation of bibliographies
Let us abandon forever
the temptation to make much of little
to scratch our initials in the dust
Let us remember stars evolve and have life histories,
death throes
and the sun our brightest star and sometime god
consumes itself at its innermost core

Let us recall of creation
there is no vestige of beginning
no adumbration of the end
By which sense can we know time, its deep interior,
our five senses cannot reach?
We measure by invisible intervals
the obedient twice-daily tides
uncountable layers of prehistory
gods creating and destroying
on the Wheel of Time.
Mountains thrust up and erode,
seas cover all.
Sands inter Pharaonic monuments
of immortality.

Let us wonder where we stand –
a many-islanded universe
every nebulous star appearing
as the firmament of some other world

universe without center, without edge
Where will the arrow of Amytas fall?
Let us recall Pascal's alarm
at the eternal silence of infinite space

All ponderable things seek to lay
their heaviness down
Newton affirming that gravity belongs to God
Let us remember that 'atom' means 'uncuttable'
and feel chagrin
Everything in a state of becoming
world of potentiality
where electrons strike scintillas of light
waves spread out and interlace

Our lives like virtual particles
may spend one brief ecstatic moment
before we die, but
even an unhappy life may be enough

ii.

The wilderness within
grown dangerous and green
edgy with wanting
strains to hear

Memling's painted angel
plucking the portative
octave by octave
down from the angelic high C

Has the soul its own pitch
like a vibrating string?

The dream of faith:
harmony of the spheres
and the Great Tuner tuning all

iii.

The universe, of which nature is the body, God the soul

Newton, in his shed at Trinity,
begins in alchemy,
conjuring vapors and spirits
working on each other,
glorying in change.
Still, he sees all things connected,
the body to the universe,
the same laws governing all:
What makes the planets dance,
the apple fall.

iv.

But what of the planets' imperfect ellipses
the wolves of discord
howling in the wilderness
forbidden notes   dangerous and green
music born of Jove and Memory

v.

We rest our souls in Plato's Meadow,
two doors into earth, two into heaven,
a bright shaft of light
stretching between
the Spindle of Necessity
turns as we climb

Time carries us from Creation to Judgment
Unmaking the body, unmaking the life

vi.

Of what is matter made
that things transform and wither?

Dust, rain, wind, flame —
combining, recombining, so as to be conserved,
eternal as we are not.
Ever more accurate, we weigh the world for proof,
the balance pole with its brass pans, oldest of our tools.

But what if matter, weighed piece by piece,
doesn't add up to a whole we can describe?
If, sailing like Ulysses from the known,
we meet chaos at the misty limits of the mind?

In Memling's painting *The Last Judgment* it's no scientist
but Michael the Archangel who does the weighing,
counts the bodies, naked and strangely small,
praying, crawling, buckling
backward before his sheathed and gleaming power.

vii.

The snowflake falls heedlessly toward dissolution
but the body knows its exits, entrances, fluidities.
Spirit rages agains the 'pain of being born into matter,'
but the body loves the delicate smell of the violets of hope.
In the Scrovegni chapel, Giotto's Mary receives a model
of the temple, tiers of angels rise behind her.
Bottom right, a gigantic Satan defecates a sinner.
Mary's blue robe glints with godly gold
like the starred barrel-vault of heaven.
Satan squats at the confluence
of the four blood-red rivers of hell.

Spirit and matter rescued in the Palladian plan.
Porticoes, pediments, pillars, sheltering barchesses
like wings on either side.
The perfect symmetry the snowflake falls to lose.

viii.

> 'Humility, the beautiful daughter
> all her ways are empty...'
>   Agnes Martin

Agnes Martin paints the innocence
of trees. Not the 'exhaustable'
passions, but a grid, spiritual space,
each square radiant as if lit
from within, each almost a prayer.
Her faint pencil lines dissolve as
you retreat, leaving a shimmer held
in equilibrium, perfect and anonymous.
No object here; works level as water.
Emptiness closer and closer to rest.

ix.

The formless needs to be concealed.
Who dares summon demons
from their dissonant intervals,
risk shipwreck through miscalculation?
Number binds the order of the soul
and of the universe.
More than our days are numbered,
children of Kronos. Speech, step, song.
One rectangle so beautiful
men call it golden,
the Divine Proportion of the Parthenon.
The light years we wait to see the light.

x.

Like the excited atoms of the candle flame
Mozart's joyful measures dance together
to give off light
by which we see
passions fitted into harmony.
Immovable was the Pallace of Faelicitye.

xi.

"Nothing will come of nothing. Try again."
King Lear

As in the darkness there are unborn stars,
so Cordelia, her just measure of devotion,
does not appear to Lear. They are two stars,
orbiting each other, his sight obscured
by clouds of dust, random deflections
of pomp and ceremony in the line of sight.

But as variable stars change their brightness,
and no star lasts forever, here's the king
deposed, despised, and wandering in his wits.
He's down to nature now, and owns
the natural affections. Who does not weep

to hear him croon a lullaby
to his youngest daughter? Star light, star bright.
So something comes of nothing. Before he dies,
Cordelia will be blest, and Lear forgiven.
So once the world was bathed with intense light,
creation never finished or complete.

xii.

Sometimes I think everything that has happened
or will happen takes place in or by the sea
and when I'm away I miss what my life is for,
where the world goes. Are those the mollusks
from which life began, flinging themselves
on the shore? Is that Ulysses curving around Ithaca,
selkies lamenting off the coast of Inverness?

O seas of green, blue, turquoise, yellow-brown,
seas of icebergs and baobab trees, triremes and slavers,
tossing the lost continent of Atlantis, the sunken city
of Lyonesse, the drowned Phoenician sailor, O seas
with bells between your flanks, tolling fathoms
down where jeweled monsters sleep: Days and their shadows,
their words, are nothing to you. So they are nothing to me,
    either.

xiii.

The night gathers and advances
and the day meekly subsides
at the horizon of the visible world
where time stands still
and when we look up into transparent space
we look backward in time
so the light of now may proceed
from a long-vanished star.

And the day is beautiful and the night, also.

Our legs will carry us and our hands
will carry for us as far
as the place of Infinite Duration,
the Eternal Abode.

I have been prepared
for the dangerous passage
through the underworld
into the second life.

My face and fingerstalls have been gilded
since the flesh of the gods in gold.
Osiris has heard my confession
at the Weighing of the Heart
and I am justified.
I have amulets tucked in my layered white linen,
ready is the canopic jar to receive my organs
leaving the body incorruptible.

On the head of my mummy case
my own portrait is painted, a semblance
of life preserved in death
so you will know me
when I look at you.

xiv.

Here are the deliberations of the heart:
the dead Christ, horizontal,
feet foremost, soles calloused
from the barefoot march to Calvary.
We see the man before the god:
sex swollen beneath draped cloth,
black luxuriant curls. The muscular torso
more stilled than frailty could be,
more fallen. I think of all the Cruxifixions
I have seen: elevated, distant, anguish
of Mary and the saints, immeasurable.
Mantegna, master of foreshortening, knew
the feet would draw us in,
make the heart consider:
There is nothing too wonderful to be true.

xv.

Zen leaves the circle,
most beautiful of forms,
incomplete, so we can feel creation.

The cloud thinning to transparency
then remembering itself denser with rain
the wind calling attention to the leaves
then the tremolo of the leaves returning attention to the wind

xvi.

Seeking order on earth, we scan the sky,
though stars cast off, planets detach from stars.
We long to find a changeless world,
to track Andromeda across the vault,
spiral of swimming stars on her left foot.
Pattern-makers, we shape what's strange,
curvature of starlight seen
as gods, animals, a milky pathway to the dead.

Nature in mathematics' net,
the dream of reason.
This god also dies.
What of randomness, the indeterminate,
we have just begun to read?
The nucleus disintegrates
and we can't measure it.
Rarely in nature
are perfect symmetries.
We enter at the flaw,
build Chartres, Mont St. Michel,
hungry for what's faultless and coheres.

The world clock turns
above the fossil earth,
silent as sidereal spheres.
Memory saves us from the isolation of the stars.

xvii.

Sometimes you shrink from touch
as if your skin were feverish sore.
As if words were beak-brutal,
and you envy the sweetmeat nuts their hard shell.
I envy the still life paintings of the Dutch,
so unafraid, so solid. More than the yellow,
the blue, the highlights of white,
the burnishing of objects that are loved.
Comfort, they say. The stone jug, the spinet,
know why they are here.

Who can bear to look these new fine –
ground lenses, peering at the near and far world?
Don't they know they're turning the world upside down,
as watery ditches reflect their vast sky,
skimming flat fields to the Zuider Zee?
And these women, some with their sleeves rolled
showing their ample arms, one playing the spinet,
one pouring from a jug, one making lace at the door,
what will happen to them
in a measureless world
where Delft burns to the ground
and Dutch ships, with their brave instruments
founder at sea?

xviii.

As brain-waves smooth out during sleep,
the sea is making calm three fathoms deep.
Making all aspects of the marvelous caught there
visible and even, like glass seen under water.

xix.

There seems an interval between notes
when time merely elapses
as in Mondrian's *Ocean and Piers*
where space buoys up the lines,
verticals, horizontals, until
the whole levitates
above its rectangular ground.
How happy we are, forsaking metaphor, to float,
abstract as we can never be.

xx.

It's not just energy, action, or even de-centering
we recognize in Jackson Pollock's painting
but the nervy agitation, jumps and starts,
anxious delivery of dribble and splash,
incomplete neurons and stars. The hand here now, there then,
error inhering. What's going where?
With no one source of light, the focus diffuses,
demanding we take in everything at once.
And we can, these canvases are us,
how we feel loopy and dotty with the substance
of shadow, without perspective.
How we feel time like scattershot seconds,
racing fugitive and scissored from the past:
Goodbye landscape, the noble subject, narratives from history.
Far behind us too, romantic and real,
'Madame Bougeeau with Red Hat,' 'Young Girl with Cat,'
and no returning. Here we are,
painted as sub-atomic particles: Uncertainty,
a modified chaos, we're managing that.

xxi.

Between the particle and the wave
the Han dancer –
reverberation of the verb
in the noun-thereness of the world

xxii.

What is negotiable in this world?
Not what we keep, not what we give away.
Not what is taken from us. So we invent
lies of stability, love the horizon's
calm repose, also a lie, that lets our failures
sink behind it like the sun.

What is beautiful and strange in the forest
is that it is both darkness and light,
like all things which become
and vanish in a ceaseless dance. This is

difficult to bear, given our tendency
to exist. Who knows the Dance knows God.
Dervishes, wild and full of grace,
whirl like suspended particles, patterns
of ecstasy. And matter dances, too.

There are iridescent clouds, virtual clouds
in the field which is always and everywhere there.
One hand of Shiva gestures, *Do Not Fear.*
With the relentless energy of all rotating things,
we lean into the stillness of deep space.

xxiii.

Perhaps we're standing on sacred dust,
needing to dance the world back into balance

before the axis tilts
and the planet falls into the sun.

Perhaps matter is composed
of superstrings tiny beyond imagining

threads of pure energy
that hold the world together

We're dazzled by the fiery haloes
of all that's possible

What we know and what we are:
dust, rain, wind, flame